UNLOCK

ALSO BY BEI DAO

POETRY

The August Sleepwalker (1990)
translated by Bonnie S. McDougall

Old Snow (1991)
translated by Bonnie S. McDougall
and Chen Maiping

Forms of Distance (1994)
translated by David Hinton

Landscape Over Zero (1996)
translated by David Hinton with Yanbing Chen

SHORT STORIES

Waves (1990)
translated by Bonnie S. McDougall
and Susette Ternent Cooke

UNLOCK

POEMS BY

BEI DAO

TRANSLATED BY
ELIOT WEINBERGER AND
IONA MAN-CHEONG

A NEW DIRECTIONS BOOK

ACKNOWLEDGMENTS

Some of the poems in this book have appeared in the following periodicals:
Autodafé, Jacket, Sulfur, Tin House.

Manufactured in the United States of America
New Directions books are printed on acid-free paper.
First published as New Directions Paperbook 901 in 2000
Published simultaneously in Canada by Penguin Books Canada Limited

Library of Congress Cataloging-in-Publication Data

Pei-tao, 1949-
[Poems. English. Selections]
Unlock / translated by Eliot Weinberger and Iona Man-Cheong
    p. cm.
ISBN 0-8112-1447-8 (pbk. : alk. paper)
    1. Pei-tao, 1949—Translations into English. I. Weinberger, Eliot.
II. Man-Cheong, Iona, 1950- III. Title.

PL2892.E525 A25 2000
895.1'152—dc21

                                    00-030571

New Directions Books are published for James Laughlin
by New Directions Publishing Corporation
80 Eighth Avenue, New York, NY 10011

目錄 CONTENTS

UNLOCK

六　月

風在耳邊說，六月
六月是張黑名單
我提前離席

請注意告別方式
那些詞的嘆息

請注意那些詮釋：
無邊的塑料花
在死亡左岸
水泥廣場
從寫作中延伸

到此刻
我從寫作中逃跑
當黎明被鍛造
旗幟蓋住大海

而忠實于大海的
低音喇叭說，六月

JUNE

Wind at the ear says *June*
June a blacklist I slipped
in time

note this way to say goodbye
the sighs within these words

note these annotations:
unending plastic flowers
on the dead left bank
the cement square extending
from writing to

now
I run from writing
as dawn is hammered out
a flag covers the sea

and loudspeakers loyal to the sea's
deep bass say *June*

閱　讀

品嘗多餘的淚水
你的星宿啊
照耀着迷人的一天

一隻手是誕生中
最抒情的部份
一個變化着的字
在舞蹈中
尋找它的根

看夏天的文本
那飲茶人的月亮
正是廢墟上
烏鴉弟子們的
黃金時間

所有跪下的含義
損壞了指甲
所有生長的煙
加入了人的諾言

品嘗多餘的大海
背叛的鹽

READING

Taste the unnecessary tears
your star stays
alit still for one charmed day

a hand is birth's
most expressive thing
a word changes
dancing
in search of its roots

read the text of summer
the moonlight from which
that person drinks tea
is the true golden age
for disciples of crows in the ruins

all the subservient meanings
broke fingernails
all the growing smoke
seeped into the promises

taste the unnecessary sea
the salt betrayed

安魂曲
　一給珊珊

那一年的浪頭
淹沒了鏡中之沙
迷途即離別
而在離別的意義上
所有語言的瞬間
如日影西斜

生命只是個諾言
別為它悲傷
花園毀滅以前
我們有過太多時間
爭辯飛鳥的含義
敲開午夜之門

孤獨象火柴被擦亮
當童年的坑道
導向可疑的礦層
迷途即離別
而詩在糾正生活
糾正詩的回聲

REQUIEM

for Shanshan

The wave of that year
flooded the sands on the mirror
to be lost is a kind of leaving
and the meaning of leaving
the instant when all languages
are like shadows cast from the west

life's only a promise
don't grieve for it
before the garden was destroyed
we had too much time
debating the implications of a bird flying
as we knocked down midnight's door

alone like a match polished into light
when childhood's tunnel
led to a vein of dubious ore
to be lost is a kind of leaving
and poetry rectifying life
rectifies poetry's echo

無　題

撫摸傷口我看到輝煌的時刻
那淬火的斧子驚醒罷工的大海
許多把鑰匙插進同一夜裡
哦燈光

裸露于大地的時間多麼沉靜
如同分開洪水的房頂
在鳥類命運中變化的氣候
被辨別月亮指紋的風所確認

投石問路，十倍于現實的書
擋住了召喚證人的叫喊
所有的疑問都指向愛
當死去的朋友浮現出笑容

UNTITLED

Rubbing this bruise I see an instant of brilliance
a slaking axe startles a sea on strike awake
all the keys are inserted in the same night
lamplight

how calm the times exposed on earth
like the rooftop that splits the floodwaters
the changing climate of the fate of birds
known by a wind that reads the fingerprints of moonlight

throw a stone to ask the way   the book ten times reality
obstructs the calling of the witnesses
all existing doubts point toward love
in the presence of a dead friend whose smile floats up

錯　誤

獨奏的薩克斯管
用雨織成夜
燈光織成廟宇
讓死水長出骨頭
四處遊動

並非沒有榮耀
我讓壞天氣
轉向玫瑰的話題
借助雙刃剃刀
檢查青春：

一張正確的臉
理髮師剪去
多餘的歲月
我看起來還行
穿過鏡子

在另一個時代
我慢慢生鏽
在我週圍
有人交易有人演講
卻沒有聲音

MISTAKE

Solo saxophone
weaves rain into night
weaves a temple into lamplight
lets dead water grow bones
that wander about

it's not that there is no honor
I let the bad weather turn
into the topic of roses
examining youth
with a double-edged razor

one proper face
the barber clips
unnecessary years
still all right
to pass a mirror

slowly rusting
in another era
around me
people doing business giving lectures
without a sound

日子與道路

陰影如船歌
穿過古老綠色
風箏在太陽左邊
是等待批准的
暴風雪

另起一段，象
拉開無夢的抽屜
所有裂縫充滿
做愛的呼吸

交通信號燈指出
日子與道路的分歧
這隱喻如染缸
浸透我們的衣裳
開始的聲音
結束的顏色

TIME AND THE ROAD

Shadows like a boat song
crossing ancient green
a kite to the left of the sun
awaits the authorized
blizzard

set up another stanza like
a dreamless drawer pulled open
all its cracks filled
with lovemaking breath

traffic light marks
the fork of time and the road
this metaphor like a vat of dye
soaks through our clothes
sound of the beginning
color of the end

送　報

誰相信面具的哭泣
誰相信哭泣的國家
國家失去記憶
記憶成為早晨

送報的孩子從早晨出發
淒厲的小號響遍全城
是你的不幸還是我的不幸
神經脆弱的蔬菜啊
農民們把手栽進地裡
盼望抓住金條的好年景
政客在自己舌頭上
撒着胡椒粉
而樺樹林正在討論
是捐軀于藝術還是門

這個公共的早晨
被送報的孩子所創造
一場革命掠過街頭
他睡着了

DELIVERING NEWSPAPERS

Who believes in the mask's weeping?
who believes in the weeping nation?
the nation has lost its memory
memory goes as far as this morning

the newspaper boy sets out in the morning
all over town the sound of a desolate trumpet
is it your bad omen or mine?
vegetables with fragile nerves
peasants plant their hands in the ground
longing for the gold of a good harvest
politicians sprinkle pepper
on their own tongues
and a stand of birches in the midst of a debate:
whether to sacrifice themselves for art or doors

this public morning
created by a paperboy
revolution sweeps past the corner
he's fast asleep

陽　臺

鐘聲是一種慾望
會導致錯誤的風向
有人沿着街道的
吩咐回家
走向他的蘋果

說書人和故事一起
遷移，沒再回來
數數鳥窩
我們常用數字
記住那赤腳的歌聲
年代就這樣
爬上我們的黃昏

剛好到陳酒斟在
杯子裡的高度
回憶忙於挑選客人
看誰先到達

BALCONY

A bell-sound is a kind of desire
that can mislead the wind
someone follows the street's
instructions to go home
to his apple

the narrator and the story
left and did not come back
to count birds' nests
we often use numbers
to remember that barefoot singing
suddenly the times
creep up on our twilight

it came to the point
of pouring old wine
memory is picking out the guests
see who arrives first

古　堡

那些玫瑰令人羞慚
象這家族的真理
讓你久久逗留

噴泉追溯到生殖
黑暗的第一線光明
死水吞吃浮雕上
驕傲的火焰

松牆的迷宮是語法
你找到出路才會說話
沿着一級級台階
深入這語言的內部
明門暗道通向
那回聲般的大廳

你高喊，沒有回聲

在環繞你的肖像中
最後一代女主人
移開她老年的面具

在情慾之杯飲水
她目送一隻貓
走出那生命的界線

THE OLD CASTLE

Those roses a cause of shame
like the truth of this clan
letting you linger for a long while

the fountain traces back the first thread of light
in the darkness of reproduction
stagnant water swallows
the arrogant flame on the carved relief

the pine hedge labyrinth is a grammar
find the way out and you can speak
follow the flight of stairs
deep into this language
unobstructed corridors and hidden passages
lead to that echoing hall

you shout out loud, there is no echo

portraits surround you
the last generation of hostesses
slip off their old-age masks

drinking water from desire's cup
her eyes carry a cat
beyond the boundaries of life

零度，琴聲蕩漾
他人的時刻表
不再到達的明天

1916: 年。戰爭箭頭
指往所有方向
她鋪上雪白的桌布
召喚飢餓的藝術
當最後的燭火
陳述着世紀的風暴
她死于飢餓

井，大地的獨眼

你觸摸燭臺
那隻冰冷的手
握住火焰
她喂養過的鴿子
在家族的沉默作窩

聽到明天的嘆息
大門砰然關閉
藝術已死去
玫瑰剛剛開放

zero degrees, sound of a piano rippling
someone else's calendar
a tomorrow that never returns

1916: the arrowheads of war
point in all directions
she spreads the white tablecloth
to invoke the art of starvation
as the light of the last candle
reports the century's storm
she dies of starvation

a well, the earth's single eye

you touch the candlestick
that frozen hand
gripping the flame
the pigeons she raised
make their nests in the clan silence

hearing the sighs of tomorrow
the main gate clangs shut
art is dead
roses bloom

無　題

小號如尖銳的犁
耕種夜:多久
陽光才會破土

多久那聆聽者才會
轉身，看到我們
多久我們才會
通過努力
成為我們的榮耀

直到谷粒入倉
這思想不屬於誰
那有此刻與來世的
落差:巨浪拍岸
我們與青春為鄰
聽狂暴心跳

在更空曠的地方
睡眠塞滿稻草

UNTITLED

A trumpet like a sharp plow
tills the night: how long
till sunlight breaks the ground?

how long till those who listen respectfully
turn around and see us?
how long till we
through effort and exertion
turn into glory?

till the grain goes into the granary
this thought belongs to no one
a drop in the water-level between
this moment and the next life:
huge waves beat against the shore
next door to youth
we hear the wild palpitations

in a space even vaster
sleep stuffed with rice straw

崗　位

一隻麋鹿走向陷阱
權力，樅樹說，鬥爭

懷着同一秘密
我頭髮白了
退休—倒退着
離開我的崗位

只退了一步
不，整整十年
我的時代在背後
突然敲響大鼓

POST

An elk heading for the pit-trap
power, the fir tree said, struggle

cherishing the same secret
my hair turned white
retiring, going backwards
leaving my post

only one step back
no, ten whole years
my era behind me
suddenly beating on a bass drum

戰　後

從夢裡蒸餾的形像
在天邊遺棄旗幟

池塘變得明亮
那失蹤者的笑聲
表明:疼痛
是蓮花的叫喊

我們的沉默
變成草漿變成
紙，那愈合
書寫傷口的冬天

POSTWAR

Images distilled from the dream
abandon the flag at the horizon

the light cast by the pond
the laughter of those missing
makes it clear: pain
is the cry of the lotus

our silence
became straw pulp became
paper, that winter
healing the written wounds

嗅覺

那氣味讓人記憶猶新
象一輛馬車穿過舊貨市場
古董、假貨和叫賣者的
智慧矇上了灰塵

和你的現實總有距離
在和老闆的爭吵中
你看見窗戶裡的廣告
明天多好，明天牌牙膏

你面對着五個土豆
第六個是洋蔥
這盤棋的結局如悲傷
從航海圖上消失

SMELLS

Those smells making you remember again
like a horse-cart passing through the flea-market
curios, fakes, hawkers'
wisdom covered in dust

and there's always a gap between you and reality
arguing with the boss
you see the ad out the window
a bright tomorrow, Tomorrow brand toothpaste

you are facing five potatoes
the sixth is an onion
the outcome of this chess game is like sorrow
disappearing from the maritime chart

開　車

旋律掙脫琴弦的激動
隨煙霧溜出車窗
加入祖父們的靈魂

早安，白房子
你這田野永遠奔忙的
救護車狂風
妄想打開的書映在
天上那電影的
忠實觀眾

醒來的人繼續着
夢中的工作
駕駛巨大的割麥機
除掉不潔的念頭

紅燈亮了：
筑路工的真理

DRIVING

The melody breaks free from the agitating strings
follows the smoke slipping out the car window
joining the spirits of the grandfathers

good morning, white house
you are an ambulance always in a hurry
in the field a book a hurricane uselessly
hope to open a loyal audience
of movies of sky

those awake keep working
in the dream
driving the giant harvester
that clears impure thoughts

the red light comes on
the truth for road workers

無　題

被筆勾掉的山水
在這裡重現

我指的絕不是修辭
修辭之上的十月
飛行處處可見
黑衣偵察兵
上昇，把世界
微縮成一聲叫喊

財富變成洪水
閃光一瞬擴展成
過冬的經驗
當我象個偽證人
坐在田野中間
大雪部隊卸掉偽裝
變成語言

UNTITLED

The landscape crossed out with a pen
reappears here

what I am pointing to is not rhetoric
October over the rhetoric
flight seen everywhere
the scout in the black uniform
gets up, takes hold of the world
and microfilms it into a scream

wealth turns into floodwaters
a flash of light expands
into frozen experience
and just as I seem to be a false witness
sitting in the middle of a field
the snow troops remove their disguises
and turn into language

不

答案很快就會知道
日曆，那撒謊的光芒
已折射在他臉上

臨近遺忘臨近
田野的旁白
臨近祖國這個詞
所擁有的絕望

麥粒飽滿
哦成熟的哭泣
今夜最忠實的孤獨
在為他引路

他對所有排隊
而喋喋不休的日子
說不

NO

The solution soon knows
the calendar, that lying radiance
already refracted in his face

close to forgetting close to
the monologues of open country
close to the homeland this word
all the despair it holds

fat grains of wheat
weep as they ripen
tonight faithful solitude
leads his way

and to all the days in line
endlessly chattering
he says No

中秋節

含果核的情人
許願，互相愉悅
直到從水下
潛望父母的嬰兒
誕生

那不速之客敲我的
門，帶着深入
事物內部的決心

樹在鼓掌

喂，請等等，滿月
和計劃讓我煩惱
我的手翻飛在
含義不明的信上
讓我在黑暗裡
多坐一會兒，好像
坐在朋友的心中

這城市如冰海上
燃燒的甲板
得救?是的，得救
水龍頭一滴一滴
哀悼着源泉

MOON FESTIVAL

Lovers holding pits in their mouths
make vows and delight in each other
till the underwater infant
periscopes his parents
and is born

an uninvited guest knocks at my
door, determined to go deep
into the interior of things

the trees applaud

wait a minute, the full moon
and this plan are making me nervous
my hand fluttering
over the obscure implications of the letter
let me sit in the dark
a while longer, like
sitting on a friend's heart

the city a burning deck
on the frozen sea
can it be saved? it must be saved
the faucet drip-drop drip-drop
mourns the reservoir

夜空

沉默的晚餐
盤子運轉着黑暗
讓我們分享
這煮熟的憤怒
再來點鹽

假設擁有更大的
空間—舞台
飢餓的觀眾
越過我們的表演
目光向上

如昇旗，升向
夜空:關閉的廣場
一道光芒指出變化
移動行星
我們開始說話

NIGHT SKY

Silent dinner
the dishes spin darkness
letting us share this
simmered anger
add a little salt

suppose there were an even greater
space — a stage
the starving spectators
looking up
at our acting

like raising a flag, rising into
the night sky: the square is shut down
a ray of light points out the changes
shifting planets
we begin to speak

無 題

被霧打濕
念頭象被寒流
抖落的鳥群
你必忍受年齡
守望田野
傾聽偉大音樂中
迂迴的小徑

而你是否會被
演奏所忽略
荒蕪呵

不，簡單
而並不多餘
那讚美
那天空與大地
在水面之吻

UNTITLED

Soaked by fog
thoughts like a flock of birds
shake out of the cold drafts
you must endure aging
watch over the fields
listen closely to the circuitous paths
through powerful music

perhaps you were ignored
by the orchestra
desolation

no, simply
not at all superfluously
that praise
that kiss on the water's surface
between sky and earth

出　門

羅盤幽默地
指向一種心境
你喝湯然後走出
這生活的場景

天空與電線的
表格上，一棵樹
激動得欲飛
又能寫些什麼

無論如何，你將
重新認識危險
一群陌生人坐在
旅行的終點

風在夜裡盜鈴
長髮新娘
象弓弦起伏在
那新郎身上

LEAVING HOME

The compass jokingly
points toward a state of mind
you drink up the soup and leave
this scene of life

on the application form of
sky and electric wires, a tree
trembling to fly
so what can it write about?

no matter what happens, you'll
recognize the danger
a crowd of strangers sitting
at journey's end

at night the wind steals bells
the long-haired bride
quivers like a bowstring
over the body of the groom

靈魂游戲

那些手梳理秋風
有港口就有人等待
晴天，太多的
麻煩彙集成烏雲

天氣在安慰我們
象夢夠到無夢的人

日子和樓梯不動
我們上下奔跑
直到藍色腳印開花
直到記憶中的臉
變成關上的門

請坐，來談談
這一年剩下的書頁
書頁以外的沉淪

SPIRIT GAME

Those hands comb autumn winds
to have a port means someone waiting
for clear skies, too many troubles
converging in a black cloud

weather comforts us
like a dream reaching the dreamless

days and staircases do not move
we run up and down them
until the blue footprints blossom
until the remembered face
becomes a closed door

have a seat, let's talk
the pages left in this year
the sinkings beyond the pages

哭 聲

大雪之蹄踏遍牧場
狂風正是騎手

歷史不擁有動詞
而動詞是那些
試着推動生活的人
是影子推動他們
並因此獲得
更陰暗的含義

一把小提琴誘導
我們轉向過去
聽人類早年的哭聲
其中有榮耀
迷途先知的不幸

讓不幸降到我們
所理解的程度
每家展開自己的旗幟
床單、炊煙或黃昏

CRYING

Hooves of heavy snow stamp the pasture
fierce wind   the horseman exactly

history has no verbs
verbs are those
trying to push life ahead
shadows push them ahead
toward even darker
implications

a violin induces us
to turn to the past
to hear the crying in mankind's early years
the honor
and misfortunes of lost prophets

let misfortune fall
on the level of our understanding
each family unfolds its banner
bedsheets, kitchen smoke, dusk

夜　樹

那否認的激情
不正來自感動嗎
深淵孤燈
指引堅信的鳥
在免疫的外省
鄰居們正修辭般
偷天換日

誰上昇誰醒來

開窗從生活的縫隙
探頭是退休者的
臨時責任
那來自遺忘的
帶薄荷味的郵差
與此刻掛鉤

夜樹穿過白天的街道

NIGHT TREE

Doesn't the passion of rejection come
from being moved?
a single lantern in the abyss
guides the way for confident birds
in the immune outer provinces
the neighbors rhetorically
steal the sky and put up a fake sun

whoever rises whoever wakes

opening the window and looking out
from the cracks of life
is temporary employment
for the retirees
the mint-flavored mailman
comes from oblivion
to connect to this moment

the night tree crosses the daylight street

教師手冊

一所尚未放學的學校
暴躁不安但克制
我睡在它旁邊
我的呼吸夠到課本
新的一課:飛行

當陌生人的驕傲
降下三月雪
樹絮根于天空
筆在紙上突圍
河的拒絕橋的邀請

上鉤的月亮
在我熟悉的樓梯
拐角，花粉與病毒
傷及我的肺傷及
一隻鬧鐘

放學是場革命
孩子們跨越光的柵欄
轉入地下
我和那些父母一起
看上昇的星星

TEACHER'S MANUAL

A school still in session
irritable restless but exercising restraint
I sleep beside it
my breath just reaching the next
lesson in the textbook: how to fly

when the arrogance of strangers
sends down March snow
a tree takes root in the sky
a pen to paper breaks the siege
the river declines the bridge invites

the moon takes the bait
turning the familiar corner
of the stairs, pollen and viruses
damage my lungs damage
an alarm clock

to be let out of school is a revolution
kids jump over the railings of light
and turn to the underground
other parents and I
watch the stars rise

練習曲

風，樹林的窮親戚
去天邊度假
向巨鐘滾動的河
投擲檸檬

攝影機追隨着陽光
象鋼琴調音
那些小小的死亡
音色純正

寫作與戰爭同時進行
中間建造了房子
人們坐在裡面
象謠言，準備出發

戒煙其實是戒掉
一種手勢
為什麼不說
詞還沒被照亮

ÉTUDE

Wind, the poor relation of the woods
goes to the horizon to spend its vacation
throwing lemons
into a river rolling with enormous bells

the camera follows the sunlight
like a piano being tuned
those little deaths
pure tone color

war and writing move onward
houses are built between them
people sit there like rumors
waiting to start out

to quit smoking is only to give up
a kind of hand gesture
why not say
words still have not been lit?

删 節

蟋蟀在荒草歌唱

蟋蟀讓人想到
死路駕馭着生者

荒草在歌唱

荒草讓人想到
對風的全民投票

歌唱

歌唱讓人想到
尋找風格的叫喊

DELETING

Crickets sing in the weeds

crickets making us think
of the dead-end road that drives the living

weeds sing

weeds making us think
of a general election about the wind

sing

singing making us think
of searching for a way of screaming

寫 信

那地址在我出生時
奔忙，貼上郵票

直到我搬家
它才變得完整

簽名，然後我
穿過夜的無言歌

多少迷途的窗戶
才能藏住一個月亮

日子，金色油漆
我們稱為恐懼

WRITING A LETTER

That address when I was born
hurried sticking stamps

till I moved
and it completed

having signed my name, I
crossed the wordless song of night

how many lost windows
can hide a moon?

the days, the gilt paint
we call fear

無 題

平面的歌手立體的歌聲
再鞠一躬，謝謝
掙脫地窖的路歡呼
紮根的觀眾結出果子
象膽結石聚集着
比愛更真實的疼痛

日夜轉換頻道
我打開寄自大海的
昂貴的水費帳單
我們的腎長在心的位置
水淌入浩蕩的睡眠
鹽變成語言

喂，夥計，時間？
現在夜裡一點
是啊，頭上是兩個季節
臨時的結盟，媽的
腳邊有花之間的鬥爭
好運氣，再見

在禁區以外抽煙
我比悲傷年輕
上樓，關燈，我目送
詩的主人離開小城
從窗口垂下床單
加入無言者的黎明

UNTITLED

Two-dimensional singer three-dimensional singing
take another bow, thank you
the road, cheering, struggles to be free from the basement
the rooted audience bears fruit
gall stones gather pain
more real than love

day and night change channels
I open an exorbitant bill
for water from the open seas
kidneys are where the heart should be
water trickles into the vastness of sleep
salt turns into language

hey pal got the time?
one in the morning
yeah right, up there the two seasons
briefly align, well fuck it,
flowers struggle beside our feet
good luck and goodbye

smoking outside the restricted zone
I am younger than melancholy
going upstairs, I switch off the lights and watch
the master of poetry leaving town
sheets hanging out the window
take part in the wordless people's dawn

懷　念

從呼吸困難的
終點轉身—
山岡上的落葉天使
屋脊起伏的大海

回到敘述途中
水下夢想的潛水員
仰望飛逝的船只
旋渦中的藍天

我們講的故事
暴露了內心的弱點
象祖國之子
暴露在開闊地上

風與樹在對話
那一瘸一拐的行走
我們圍攏一壺茶
老年

IN MEMORY

Turning back from the end
when it was hard to breathe —
the angels of fallen leaves on the hill
the sea of heaving rooftops

on the way back to the story
the deep-sea diver in the dream
looks up at the ships passing by
blue sky in the whirlpools

the tale we are telling
exposes the weakness in our hearts
like the sons of the nation
laid out on the open ground

dialogue of wind and trees
a limp
we crowd around a pot of tea
old age

透明度

鏡子的學問
——變化
來訪者們
使家園更荒涼

而我的旁白
如守夜者的額頭
開始發亮

三隻鳥改變了
天空的憂鬱

TRANSPARENCY

The mirror's erudition
transforms
its visitors
the homeland becomes even more desolate

and yet my monologues
like the foreheads of night watchmen
begin to shine

three birds transfigure
the night's melancholy

代 課

沉船和第六街退休的
將軍因阻擋過風暴而嗜睡
我被辭退，一封信
帶着權威的數字
讓我承認他們的天空
是的，我微不足道
我的故事始于一個輪子

白樺林整齊的弓弦
一起搭向駿馬的脖頸
游說于地圖的歧路
穿過記憶時染上了顏色
圖書館已關門
那些被分類的證人
等待着逆時針的愛情

我為一位老師代課
她到叢林去生一本書
我扑向比書更大的黑板
鳥在其中藏起糧食
窗外，草地發藍
從賣氣球的人那裡
每個孩子牽走一個心願

SUBSTITUTE-TEACHING

Sinking ships and the retired general on Sixth Street
like to sleep to quell the storms
I was fired, a letter
bearing authoritative figures
forced me to acknowledge their heaven
it's true, I'm not worth mentioning
my story began on a wheel

the white birches' tidy rows of bowstrings
come together on the stallion's neck
branch roads canvassing the map
are tinted as they cut through memory
the library's closed
cataloged witnesses
wait for counterclockwise love

I substitute for a teacher
who's gone into the forest to give birth to a book
I throw myself at a blackboard bigger than a book
where birds have hidden seeds
outside the window, the lawns grow green
from the balloon man
every kid carries a wish away

晨　歌

詞是歌中的毒藥

在追蹤歌的夜路上
警笛回味著
夢游者的酒精

醒來時頭疼
像窗戶透明的音箱
從沉默到轟鳴

學會虛度一生
我在鳥聲中飛翔
高叫永不

當風暴加滿汽油
光芒抓住發出的信
展開，再撕碎

MORNING SONG

Words are the poison in a song

on the track of the song's night road
police sirens   aftertaste
the alcohol of sleepwalkers

waking up, a headache
like the window's transparent speakers
from silence to a roar

learning to waste a life
I hover in the birdcalls
crying never

when the storms have filled up with gas
light rays snatch the letter
unfold it and tear it up

目的地

你沿著奇數
和練習發音的火花
旅行，從地圖
俯瞰道路的葬禮
他們挖得真深
觸及詩意

句號不能止住
韻律的陣痛
你靠近風的隱喻
隨白髮遠去
暗夜打開上頜
露出樓梯

DESTINATION

You follow the odd numbers
the sparks practicing their pronunciation
you travel, looking down from the map
at the funeral of the paths
dug deep
to reach the poetry

punctuation cannot stop
the bitter pain of rhyming
you lean closer to the wind's metaphor
with white hair taking you far
black night opens its jaws
to reveal a flight of stairs

變　形

我背對窗外田野
保持著生活的重心
而五月的疑問
如暴力影片的觀眾
被烈酒照亮

除了五點鐘的蜜
早上的情人正老去
他們合為一體
哦鄉愁大海上的
指南針

寫作與桌子
有敵意的對角線
星期五在冒煙
有人沿著梯子爬出
觀眾的視野

DEFORMATION

My back to the window of open fields
holding on to the gravity of life
and the doubts of May
like the audience at a violent movie
lit by drink

except for the honey-drop at five o'clock
the morning's lovers grow old
and become a single body
a compass needle
on a homesick sea

between writing and the table
a diagonal enemy line
Friday in the billowing smoke
someone climbs a ladder
out of sight from the audience

過　夜

一條河把鱒魚帶到盤中
燒酒兄弟和高粱父親
留我過夜，玻璃
有兇手的皺紋

旅館接待員盯著我
我聽見他心臟的雜音
那心臟忽明忽暗
照亮登記表

光滑的大理石上
鋼琴曲走調
電梯把哈欠變成叫喊
穿過燈光的泡沫

風從舒展的袖子
亮出鐵拳

SPENDING THE NIGHT

A river brings a trout to the plate
brother alcohol and father sorghum
ask me to spend the night, the glass
has the wrinkles of a murderer

the hotel clerk stares at me
I hear his arrhythmic heart
that heart now bright now dim
lighting the registration form

on the glossy marble
the piano goes out of tune
the elevator turns a yawn into a scream
as it cuts through lamplit foam

coming out of its sleeve
the wind bares an iron fist

回　家

回家，當妄想
收回它的一縷青煙
我的道路平行於
老鼠的隱私

往事令我不安
它是閃電的音叉
伏擊那遺忘之手的
隱密樂器

而此刻的壓力
來自更深的藍色
拐過街角我查看
天書和海的印刷術

我看見我回家
穿過那些夜的玩具
在光的終點
酒杯與呼喊重合

GOING HOME

Going home, useless hope
takes back its wisp of smoke
my road runs parallel
to the privacy of a mouse

the past makes me anxious
it is a tuning fork of lightning
that hidden instrument
trapping a forgotten hand

yet the pressure of this moment
comes from a deeper blue
turning the corner I examine
heaven's book and the printing of the sea

I watch myself going home
passing those nighttime toys
where brightness ends
shouting and wine glasses coincide

召　喚

早晨被戰慄的鳥群發明
桃樹得出多汁的結論
被群山誇獎的女人
用光線縫紉大海

鐘聲起飛越過早晨
夠到那些頭頂
驀然轉身，我們
時間的否認者
記憶的養蠍人
為浩大悲風演奏的
街頭音樂家

追問在哪兒轉身
變成回答
在這禁忌之年
一只烏鴉單腳站著：
他的寫作經驗

為甚麼書是喧囂的？
因為憤怒的結論

CALL

Early morning invented by shivering birds
the peach tree comes to juicy conclusions
women praised by the hills
sew up the sea with rays of light

a bell-sound takes off across the morning
reaches the tops of our heads
and we turn around
deniers of the times
scorpion breeders of memory
and the street musician on the corner
playing to the vast melancholic wind

where the question turns around
to become an answer
in this forbidden year
a crow stands on one leg:
his writing experience

why do books make such a racket?
the anger of their conclusions

逆光時刻

閃電照在罪犯臉上
爭論如此激烈！
而他的足音
隨剛寫下的詩句消失

夜是個旋渦
沉睡者如一件件衣服
在洗衣機裡翻轉

一只蝴蝶翻飛在
歷史巨大的昏話中
我愛這時刻
像晾衣繩通向過去
和刮風的明天

A MOMENT AGAINST THE LIGHT

Lightning lights the criminal's face
their fierce contention
and yet his footsteps
disappear with a line of poetry just written

night is a whirlpool
deep sleepers like clothes turning over
in the washing machine

a butterfly flutters
among the huge dark words of history
I love this moment
like a clothesline leading to the past
where tomorrow's wind is blowing

狩 獵

女教師早已褪色
卻在殘缺的日記中
穿針引線
沿不斷開方的走廊
全班追趕着兔子
誰剝下它的皮?

後門通向夏天
橡皮永遠擦不掉
轉變成陽光的虛線
兔子靈魂低飛
尋找投胎人

這是個故事，很多年
有人豎着耳朵

偷看了一眼天空
我們，吮吸紅燈的狼
已長大成人

THE HUNT

The teacher faded long ago
yet the fragments of her diary
act as a go-between
following the corridors of continual evolution
the whole team chases the rabbit
who will skin it?

the back door leads to summer
the eraser can never erase
the dotted lines turning into sunlight
the rabbit's soul flies low
looking for its next incarnation

this is a story, many years ago
someone's ears pricked up

stole a glimpse of the sky
and we the wolves suckling on a red lamp
have already grown up

罌粟夜

夜與晝，象汽車
停在停車場
風攪動着謊言
與真理一邊境上
對峙的野蠻人

我走在這邊境上
好像編寫字典
為了再次確定含義
我凝視男孩
瞳孔中的馬蜂窩

擴音器在播放
那三百年前的嘆息
留下的轟鳴
嘆息者不斷縮小
變成開關

打開滿天星光
流浪者手持罌粟
尋找替換他的影子
這城市的保險箱
鎖着一個劇場

歌手失去他的喉嚨
好像聽眾聾了

POPPY NIGHT

Night and day, like a car
parked in a lot
wind stirs the lies
and truths—on the border
barbarians face off

I walk along this border
as if compiling a dictionary
fixing the meanings again
I stare at the wasps' nest
in a boy's eye

amplifiers transmit
sighs from the roaring
of three hundred years ago
and he who sighs grows smaller
turning into a dial

switching on the starlit sky
the wanderer holding a poppy
searches for the shadows that will replace him
a theater is locked
in the municipal vault

the singer loses his voice
as if the audience had become deaf

和小偷坐在一起
燈光失去記憶
好像是牛奶

我替換那流浪者
從飢餓中歸來
開燈，牛奶變質
我認出這唯一歡樂
兩歲時的愛情

我知道明天早上
修理工將等在門口
帶來他的風景
在開門時替換我
走進書中

and a thief was sitting among them
lamplight has lost its memory
as if it were milk

I stand in for that wanderer
returning from hunger
turning on the light, the milk's gone bad
I only recognize a single joy
love at two year's old

I know tomorrow morning
the repairman will wait in the doorway
then take the scenery with him
at opening time he'll replace me
walking into this book

剪 接

定格象死亡握住的杯子
導演喝了口水
轉向觀眾：
嘿，我說你去哪兒

五號公路。我開車
在沿途田鼠的視野中
架起明亮的電線

莫扎特船長
帶我穿過鄉愁洪水
太陽海蟄漂浮
高音釣的魚吐鉤
到低音區產卵

導演用喇叭叫喊
隔着很多世紀

我問路問天
問一位死去詩人
所痴迷的句法
答曰:我僅受僱于
一陣悲風

翻書才有晝夜
馬蹄匆匆

MONTAGE

A freeze-frame is like death gripping a glass
the director drinks some water
and turns to the audience:
hey, where are you going?

Highway #5. I drive
through a field mouse's panorama
propped-up shining cables

Captain Mozart
takes me through the floodwaters of nostalgia
sunlit anemones float
a fish caught by a high note spits out a hook
at a low note she spawns

the director shouts through his megaphone
separated by countless centuries

I ask the way, ask heaven
ask a dead poet
what syntax obsesses him
he replies: I am employed only
by the melancholic wind passing by

there can be day and night   you leaf through the book
horses' hooves quickly quickly

在石板加深印記
小城貼滿電影海報:
導演在微笑

住下，大雪落進
古老的房間
樓梯繞着我的脊椎
觸及正在夜空
染色的鐘

直到鐘聲響徹全城

眾神探頭窗外
我隻身混進歷史
混進人群
圍觀一場雜耍

雜耍人就是導演
五個紅球在雙手間
流星般轉動

leave tracks on the flagstones
movie posters are pasted all over town
the director smiles

settling down, heavy snow falls
in an ancient room
a staircase winds around my spine
touching a tinted bell
in the night sky

bell-sounds penetrate the whole town

gods crane their heads out the window
alone I infiltrate history
infiltrate the crowd
standing around watching a show

the performer is the director himself
five red balls between a pair of hands
the meteor ship revolves

使　命

牧師在禱告中迷路
一扇通風窗
開向另一個時代:
逃亡者在翻牆

氣喘吁吁的詞引發
作者的心臟病
深呼吸，更深些
抓住和北風辯論的
槐樹的根

夏天到來了
樹冠是地下告密者
低語是被蜂群螫傷的
紅色睡眠
不，一場風暴

讀者們紛紛爬上岸

MISSION

The priest gets lost in prayer
an air shaft
leads to another era:
escapees climb over the wall

panting words evoke
the author's heart trouble
breathe deep, deeper
grab the locust tree roots
that debate the north wind

summer has arrived
the treetop is an informer
murmurs are a reddish sleep
stung by a swarm of bees
no, a storm

readers one by one clamber onto the shore

轉 椅

我走出房間
象八音盒裡的陰影
太陽的馬臀搖晃
在正午站穩

轉椅空空
從寫作漏斗中
有人被白紙過濾：
一張褶皺的臉
險惡的詞

關於忍受自由
關於借光

心，好像用于照明
更多的盲人
往返于晝夜間

SWIVEL CHAIR

I walk out of a room
like a shadow from a music box
the rump of the sun sways
stopping dead at noon

empty empty swivel chair
in the funnel of writing
someone filters through the white paper:
wrinkled face
sinister words

in regard to enduring freedom
in regard to can I have a light

the heart, as if illuminating
even more of the blind
shuttles between day and night

開　鎖

我夢見我在喝酒
杯子是空的

有人在公園讀報
誰說服他到老到天邊
吞下光芒?
燈籠在死者的夜校
變成清涼的茶

當記憶斜坡通向
夜空，人們淚水渾濁
說謊—在關鍵詞義
滑向劊子手一邊

滑向我：空房子

一扇窗戶打開
像高音C穿透沉默
大地與羅盤轉動
對着密碼—
破曉!

UNLOCK

I dreamt I was drinking wine
the glass was empty

someone reads a newspaper in the park
who persuades him in old age
to swallow light on the horizon?
the lamps at the night school of the dead
turn into cold tea

as the slopes of memory lead
to the night sky, tears turn muddy
people tell lies—at the crux of meaning
they slip alongside the executioner

slip alongside of me: empty house
a window opens
like a high C piercing the silence
earth and compass spin
through the secret combination—
daybreak!

寂靜與戰慄
　　　—給 B. Breytenbach

你畫下你自己
誕生—光線昇起
翻動紙夜

你釋放的瘋狂
是鑄造寂靜的真理
驕傲如內傷閃爍
使話語暗淡

在秘密的戰慄中
那些私立學校
穿制服的天使們
變成魚，質問大海

風閱讀車轍
向疼痛以外的藍絲綢
致敬

SILENCE AND TREMBLING

for B. Breytenbach

You draw yourself
being born—light rays rise
turning over paper night

the madness you set free
is the deep silence cast by truth
pride like the glittering of internal wounds
makes words grow dim

secretly trembling
those uniformed angels
from private school
turn into fish, interrogate the sea

wind reads the ruts in the road
paying tribute to the pain
beyond blue silk

旱　季

最初是故鄉的風
父親如飛鳥
在睡意朦朧的河上
突然轉向
而你已沉入霧中

如果記憶醒著
像天文臺裡的夜空
你剪掉指甲
關門開門
朋友難以辨認

直到往日的書信
全部失去陰影
你在落日時分傾聽
一個新城市
在四重奏中建成

DRY SEASON

First it's the wind from home
the father like a bird flying
over a river of drowsy haze
suddenly changes course
but you're already sunk in the fog

supposing memory wakes
like the night sky in an observatory
you clip your fingernails
close the door open the door
friends are hard to recognize

until letters from the old days
completely lose their shadows
at sunset you listen closely
to a new city
built by a string quartet

第五街

白日是發明者花園
背後的一聲嘆息
沉默的大多數
和鐘聲一起扭頭

我沿第五街
走向鏡中開闊地
侍者的心
如拳頭般攥緊

又是一天
噴泉沒有疑問
先知額頭的閃電
變成皺紋

一縷煙指揮
龐大的街燈樂隊
不眠之夜
我向月光投降

FIFTH STREET

The white sun is the sound of a sigh
behind the inventor's garden
the silent majority
turn their heads at the tolling bell

I walk down Fifth Street
toward the mirror of open fields
the hearts of waiters
like clenched fists

it's another day
the fountain has no doubts
the lightning on the prophet's forehead
turns into wrinkles

a wisp of smoke conducts
an orchestra of streetlights
sleepless night
I surrender to the moonlight

護城河

河水在我心中延伸
有多少燕子
如謙卑學者加入
這天地間?

一排椅子
開始夜的旅行
我逃學
從十二個時辰
卸下磨盤

如今我老了
像柳樹沉入夢中
城門為了遺忘
永遠敞開

蘋果鍍金
女人不再戀愛
詞是誘餌
雲中偉大的死者
在垂釣我們

MOAT

River stretching in my heart
how many swallows
like modest scholars link
sky and earth?

a row of chairs
starts out on its night journey
I cut class
to unload millstones
from the hours of the day

old now
I'm like a willow sinking into dreams
the city gate opens
to forget

a gilded apple
women will never love again
words are bait
up in the clouds the illustrious dead
fish for us

肥 皂

我在廚房洗手
肥皂水流進下水道
好像法國號的
一段心事

新娘揮手告別
赴約的運河
誰是逆流而上的
白髮證人?

與太陽合影
我的臉被遮去一半
另一半是白晝
在無風的寂寞中

魚相忘於江湖
夜創造臨時的神
吸毒者眼中的蝙蝠
正毀於激情

SOAP

In the kitchen washing my hands
soapy water runs down the drain
like a French horn's
anxiety

the bride waves goodbye
to the canal of keeping dates
who is the white-haired witness
going upstream?

a group photo with the sun
half my face covered
the other half daylight
in the windless solitude

in the rivers and lakes fish forget one another
the night creates a momentary god
bats in the eyes of drug addicts
destroy themselves in passion

A NOTE ON THE TRANSLATION

Bei Dao is the contemporary Chinese poet most widely translated in the West, and he has been fortunate in his English-language translators: Bonnie McDougall (working with Chen Maiping) for the early poems and David Hinton (with Chen Yanbing) for the more complex later work. Hinton was not available for this book, and Bei Dao persuaded me past great reluctance to try.

Although my qualifications here are slight, this was not quite the usual collaboration of a native speaker and a writer-translator who knows nothing of the language. I had spent most of my twenties studying Chinese; the fundamentals remained, though many words had drifted away in the intervening years. Bei Dao is a close friend, and I had read the McDougall and Hinton translations for him numerous times at public events; I knew the work better than most. As my collaborator, I enlisted Iona Man-Cheong, who was ideal in this role for two reasons beyond her intelligence and perceptiveness: born and raised in England, educated in Beijing, she naturally understood subtleties of difference that are often lost to those collaborators for whom English is a late second language; and, as a historian (but enthusiastic reader of poetry) she had no particular agenda for how a poem should be written—a frequent source of tension in collaborations. Besides rescuing me from the holes in my vocabulary, she prepared *pinyin* transliterations that facilitated dictionary work, for looking up a Chinese word one cannot pronounce is a tedious process. Finally, Bei Dao repeatedly checked the translations, illuminating obscurities, correcting mistakes, and resolving the problems of such things as number and tense, which are unspecified in Chinese but must be made concrete in English. Translation provides a new reading of one's own work, and in a few cases he decided to change the meaning of his original.

Bei Dao was born in 1949, the same year as the People's Republic, and he is a product of the Cultural Revolution: his college years were spent in the countryside building roads and bridges and working as a blacksmith. In the early 1970's, he and a group of young poets began writing in a way that was a conscious rejection of the folkloric and socialist realist literature that had been required by Mao Zedong since his famous speech in Yan'an in 1942. (Though Mao, who wrote classical poems, made an exception for himself.) Their models were the translations written by an older generation of Chinese modernists who were not allowed to publish their own work, but who could translate poets with the proper political credentials—such as Lorca, Neruda, Alberti, Éluard, and Aragon—even though this work was radically different from officially accepted content and form. Curiously, and quite coincidentally, many of these same European and Latin American poets were, at this same moment, important influences on a new generation of American poets.

The poetry these young Chinese poets wrote was imagistic, subjective, and often surreal. Although it had no overt political content, its assertion of individual sentiments and perceptions, of imagination itself, was considered subversive in a collectivist society. In 1978, their work became a kind of poetic conscience for the student demonstrators of the Democracy Movement. Bei Dao's "The Answer" with its simple and impassioned line, "I–do–not–believe!" was the movement's "Blowin' in the Wind," and it was reproduced on countless wall posters. The new poetry, published in China's first *samisdat* magazine, *Jintian* [Today], edited by Bei Dao, was officially denounced during the so-called Anti-Spiritual Pollution Campaign as *menglong*. (The word literally means "misty," but it does not have the same saccharine connotations in Chinese as it does in English: "obscure" or "vague" would be more exact.) *Jintian* was effectively shut down, but the young poets ironically and enthusiastically embraced *menglong* as the name for their movement.

"Obscure"—or, as it was known in the West, "Misty"—poetry would remain the primary expression for the change of consciousness yearned for by the next generation of student demonstrators, those who occupied Tiananmen Square in 1989. I recall an interview with Wuer Kaixi, one of the student leaders, some months after the government massacre that ended the protest movement and sent many into prison and exile. Wuer, a largely uneducated peasant from the far west of China who had been given a scholarship to attend Beijing University, was asked where he had found his political ideas. He replied, "I got them from reading the poetry of Bei Dao."

Bei Dao himself happened to be in Europe giving readings at the time of the massacre. He knew that he could not return, and he has been in exile ever since, for many years in various countries of northern Europe (where, as he wrote, he had to speak Chinese to the mirror) and more recently in the United States. For seven of those years his wife and young daughter were not allowed to join him. In 1990, *Jintian* was revived as a forum for the Chinese diaspora, and it continues under Bei Dao's editorial direction. At this writing, while many of the other exiled writers have been given permission to visit or return, Bei Dao is still barred from China, a threat to 1.2 billion people, and his poetry cannot be published there.

Bei Dao is not the same poet that he was in his "Obscure" days. His work has grown increasingly complex, partially owing to his discovery, in exile, of the poetries of Paul Celan and César Vallejo. Yet, like other poets who became famous young, the appreciation of his work remains frozen in the early writing. This has led to two lines of criticism that reach the same conclusion by entirely contradictory arguments. On one side, because the early work was relatively simple, and written (unbeknownst to him) under the influence of the same foreign poets who were decisive for the young American poets of the 1970's, some Western critics have charged that his is a kind of airport poetry, written for translation in an easily digestible, international style. (This, of course, completely ignores the poetry he has been writing for the past twenty years.) On the other side, there are Chinese critics who maintain that where his work once spoke directly to the people — yesterday's obscurity has apparently become today's transparency — it is now deliberately difficult in order to appeal to sophisticated Western poetry-readers. (The argument, again, is that he is writing for translation.) In the name of a more accessible and "Chinese" poetry, a new generation of poets is producing the kind of anecdotal, autobiographical poetry common to American creative writing schools; ironically, it is these nationalists who are working in the true current "international style."

Having now actually translated Bei Dao's poetry, I read these charges in amazement. If he is writing with an eye toward potential translations, he must believe in the omnipotence of translators. His poetry is full of abrupt changes in register, bits of daily or bureaucratic speech, and oblique or ironic references to classical Chinese literature, Maoist dogma, and contemporary events. One of his favorite gestures, modeled perhaps on the Japanese *renga*, seems natural in Chinese, but travels poorly: line B completes line A, but is also the beginning of a phrase or thought that is completed by line C.

Curiously, it is this complexity that links Bei Dao, a radical modern, to classical Chinese. Thanks to the great translations by Burton Watson, Kenneth Rexroth, Gary Snyder, and their followers, our image of the Chinese classics is that of a poetry that is straightforward, unadorned, relaxed, and colloquial. In fact, classical Chinese poetry is almost impossibly dense, requiring multiple readings to unravel meanings. Bei Dao's poems, like those of the late T'ang poets (particularly Li Ho and Li Shang-yin) cannot be paraphrased; they are mysteries composed of strange and arresting images and snatches of speech.

In the terrible twentieth century, there were those who spoke plainly of what they saw, and those who tried to invent a new language to express it. Bei Dao clearly belongs to the latter group. His poems are not about the Cultural Revolution, exile, or the continuing repression of intellectuals in an economically unfettered China. These are, rather, the exterior events, the surrounding world, for one of the most intensely interior poets in contemporary world poetry.

—Eliot Weinberger,
April 2000

ELIOT WEINBERGER is the author of *19 Ways of Looking at Wang Wei* and three collections of essays published by New Directions: *Works on Paper*, *Outside Stories*, and *Karmic Traces*. Among his many translations of the work of Octavio Paz are *Collected Poems 1957-1987*, *Sunstone*, and *A Tale of Two Gardens*. His edition of Jorge Luis Borges' *Selected Non-Fictions* received the National Book Critics Circle prize for criticism. In 1992 he was given the first PEN/Kolovakos Award for his work in promoting Hispanic literature in the United States, and in 2000 he was the first American literary writer to be awarded the Order of the Aztec Eagle by the government of Mexico.

IONA MAN-CHEONG is an Associate Professor of History at the State University of New York/Stony Brook and the author of *The Class of 1761: Examinations, State, and Elites in Late Imperial China*, forthcoming from Stanford University Press.

New Directions Paperbooks—A Partial Listing

For a complete listing request free catalog from
New Directions, 80 Eighth Avenue, New York 10011   †Bilingual

For a complete listing request free catalog from
New Directions, 80 Eighth Avenue, New York 10011　†Billing